Goddess Empowerment:

Discover Your Dark Feminine Power for Success

(Nadia Arain)

Lessons from the Goddess: Using Dark Feminine Power for Success

ISBN 10: 1977667368

ISBN 13: 9781977667366

Acknowledgements

I am grateful to God and Goddess for allowing this book to flow through me, as a Divine Vessel. I wish to create all the wonderful Spirits who assist me including Rosie and Belvia as well as Goddess Innana featured in this book, whom I affectionately refer to as "Princess", in my Goddess Ritualistic workings. I am deeply thankful for the tribe of awakened conscious Divine Masculine and Feminine women who have supported me, endlessly. Through their work, I have evolved into a Dark Feminine Goddess and able to serve the world at large.

Table of Contents

Foreword

Now you have the tools to start embracing your Dark Feminine, discovering your feminine energy and applying it to your life. There's so much to learn from each of these goddesses, so many opportunities to channel what they have and use that energy and knowledge to prepare for the future. Study always, seek regular improvements and never compromise your self-worth. Use the dark feminine to enhance your sexuality, return to the wild, never be ashamed of who you are. Open yourself up as the vessel you are and wait to be filled with knowledge, power, and money. Keep yourself and those you love safe and independent by becoming a strong-willed, dark Goddess yourself.

Introduction

Throughout history, in all of the most successful period of time, littered amongst the most successful civilizations on this planet, there have been strong feminine rulers. Strong Feminine Goddesses whom were powerful and inspired others, whose willingness to face the darkness, inspired others to face their own duality and find their way into the light. Perhaps one of the most interesting parts of any study of History, is that you will find an overlap amongst the religious aspects.

The gods and goddesses from various civilizations share similar qualities as they are all the same. They are simply represented by different interpretations from various civilizations. Greek tales, Roman legends, Egyptian stories all symbolize the same strong, Dark Feminine powers through their own Feminine Goddesses. Today, with access to so much information we, as women, **must come back to these roots,** must examine the true power that these goddesses gave to the women of their time, and embrace the spirit of these Goddesses, into our lives, to bring us the same Divine Empowerment and Justice. The spirit of the Dark Goddess wishes for True Divine Sexuality, Empowerment and Justice for women. Dark goddesses are all known to be the protectors of the Feminine, highly sexual and comfortable with wealth. Learning from them, embracing them, honouring them, will bring you the power you need to derive success in all things.

The Dark Goddess Today

The Dark Goddess is on the rise. Women around the world are hearing, the sacred inner call that they feel rising deep within them, to reclaim each and every one of our Sacred Feminine gifts. By awakening this Divine Sensuality, creativity, and beauty, women just like yourself, can nourish your soul and bloom as a woman. Taking the blessing of these gifts means, you have to give something back. It would be selfish to accept gifts from anyone without showing gratitude. **We must honor the dark Goddess.**

The Dark Goddess is bold, fearless, and mysterious, represented by Goddess Empowerment. Like the Spirit of Goddess Lilith, as well as Goddesses Sekhmet, Inanna and Kali. Each of these are protectors of the Feminine, highly sexual and comfortable with wealth. Just like women, the Goddess is a multidimensional individual, graceful and unapologetic whilst embodying dark and light. The Goddesses invite us to do the same. Her wisdom shows us that only by facing ourselves, can we truly find our way back to full feminine empowerment and wholeness. In fact, these Goddesses are unafraid to face the shadows of situations unknown, and from that they are powerful enough to take on the greatest transformations. Working with these goddesses on both a personal and professional level, leads to some of the greatest breakthroughs, often after the biggest breakdowns. As we invoke the Goddess in every aspect she has to bless our lives, uplift us, and heal us, we can be empowered during our most difficult times.

Becoming a Queen of Earth and Heaven with Inanna

Inanna, the Sumerian Goddess of war and love, means "Queen of Heaven".

Known as the first daughter of the moon as well as the morning and evening star, she is linked to the planet Venus the same way that Aphrodite is. She is a love goddess.

Legend shows that she is a woman of powerful sexuality. She descended into the underworld in a journey similar to that which the goddess Ishtar had to take in the future. She willingly chose to go to the underworld, so that she could learn from the wisdom of death and rebirth. She teaches us the lessons of willingly facing the darkness and accepting the dark aspects in our lives in order to learn from them. In order for her to be released from death ,she had to choose a substitute. She chose her husband who had yet to mourn the fact that she was absent when she went to the underworld. Her story about her Heiros Gamos, in the Babylonian tales with shepherd-man turned husband, Dumuzi, puts a spin on how a Goddess' heart truly reflects a woman's, passion. She found her consort in Dumuzi, after King Gilgamesh rejected marrying her, after learning of "free-loving" ways.

Passionate, full of overwhelming love which she demands of everyone who loves her in return, for love is tempered with forgiveness and compassion. There's so much that we might learn from this beautiful Goddess about tempering our deepest loves, so we do not hurtle ourselves into a destructive end. It is great to be passionate about all things whether it's a lover, child, music, or even a painting but we must face the darkness to learn what it has to teach us.

Innana is an incredible and fascinating Goddess, and very much connected to Lilith, whom we shall explore further along as our next Goddess, in terms of passion, lust and sexuality. Innana rules over fertility and many young Priestesses carried out sacred sex magick rituals to consecrate the land, to reap a bountiful harvest.

Facing Your Dark Sexuality with Lilith

Lilith is a Sumerian demon goddess, known for her roles in Jewish legends and her name of "Maiden of Desolation". Goddess Lilith is a creature of the night depicted on play plaques is a beautiful winged woman with the claws in feet of the bird.

Inanna, a Sumerian goddess of war and love, planted a sacred *huluppu* tree. She wanted to plant this tree so that she could one day carve out of it, the wood and her bed. The Brown represented the power as a female in her bed represented her full sexuality. But Lilith took up residence in this tree, symbolizing her fears. Later, as we come to realise, Goddess Lilith made friends with Innana, and Innana chose her as her sacred Handmaiden. Lilith was assigned the job, of priestess recruiting, to seduce men, to come into the Temple to have sex with them. This is the ancient art of Sacred Prostitution, something the world of today is so unfamiliar with. Men would leave coins in the Temple, as an honour for the Goddess after having sex, which was very different to paying the Priestess directly.

Lilith was Adam's first wife in the Jewish legend and she did not have sex with them so that she would not be beneath him. Lilith spoke and always speaks for TRUE Feminine Embodiment, the right to be seen as heard equally to a man.

Her tale speaks of being first. It speaks of the names that men have bestowed upon her, vampire, succubus, screech or, and clarifies that you should not listen to these terms because they have been perverted. As Patriarchy has perverted sex, so they have made women feel ashamed and dirty for their very natural, sexual desire.

She embodies the ancient and sacred name for a feathered owl, soft as snow. It is Lilith who is the darkness which balances the light. It is Lilith who makes wisdom from this balance. In her garden, that is the heart of the world grows the tree of wisdom. This garden and the tree were crafted by female, by Lilith herself, not a male God. The fruit of this tree nourishes humanity and provides the wisdom and knowledge essential for the world.

It is true, she states, that knowledge can be bitter and sweet but you have to taste the truth in order to cultivate growth. That is the reason why she created the garden. Goddess Lilith offered the apple to Eve, from a place of Sisterhood and not malice. She hoped Eve would bite into it, and see Adam for what he truly was. A domineering, patriarchal and emotionally abusive man, expecting a woman to always submit to his authority, only. Lilith prayed that Eve too, could lead a life of True Empowerment, and this is why so many religious texts, omit her name.

She would not be obedient or abused.

Known in Jewish folklore as a succubus, the sexual demon, she is revered as an independent and strong Goddess. She is completely confident in her dark and sexual powers. She refused to be subordinate to her husband and therefore willingly left Paradise rather than submit to a man who did not respect her and her Divinity. Indicative of tension and an underlying dark fear that we have to face, the Goddess Lilith always embodies a strong undercurrent of sexuality that you must recognize and helps you to face your underlying dark fears in order to become a stronger and more independent woman.

She was there at the beginning. In her tale, she speaks about the true origins of the beginning. She reviews the newer version where life became death, where knowledge was a curse, and where women were sin. The pleasure and brightness were beaten into people so that they were to eat away at their soul like a cancer. This new religion springing forth out of Adam made, sweet and innocent sex forbidden, yet humanity acknowledged it as irresistible. When a man inevitably succumbs to this sweet and innocent sex, it is expected, however the women are damned for being beautiful and seductive. Humanity was severed from the Divine and any thirst for knowledge was punished. This is what made life full of pain and longing. This is what divided the world into black and white and set humanity into war of the Male-Female rift.

It is Goddess Lilith who says she would weep about what happens to the world were she not so angry. The paradise which humanity inhabits, this earth, is good and beautiful and divine. Women who carry the seed of life and rebirth are made into slaves placed beneath men but Lilith will not let this continue. She is wonderful to summon a Sisterhood relationship with, one who will heal your wounds and tear your tears into Triumph.

Wade into the Underworld with Persephone

Persephone also was an Earth Goddess Mother during the Spring and the Summer, during which, she would guide souls into the afterlife. During the Fall/Autumn and Winter, she was the wife of Hades and the Queen of the underworld. Persephone effortlessly navigated between the dark and the light always maintaining a perfect balance. It was Persephone who reminded women of the time and, today no matter how bountiful or barren, Grace is found in every season and every time in our lives.

When we descend into the Winter of our lives (dark night of the soul), it is Persephone who invites us not to be afraid, however to delve into the darkest recesses of our unconscious self to discover our inner underworld. She demonstrates to us that no matter how harshly we might be forced into the unknown, we will transcend that victim mentality and we would become victorious. Persephone's tales are not happy ones. She was abducted and she was sadly sexually abused as well as being forced into a marriage with Hades, long before she became a beloved wife and queen. She faced some of the worst of the darkness that a woman can, but she overcame all of it. She is a true testament to the Strength and Courage that Goddess Empowerment, teaches us.

In order for us to draw on the grace and resilience that Persephone had, in our own lives as women, we must allow ourselves to face those deepest depths of our fears and what causes pain in order to achieve the greatest healing and experience all of our feelings of full force.

Consider this: most people don't realize that women and men become calmer and less selfish as they age. The reason for this is because the depth of their feelings grow as well as life experience that allows them to typically transcend the shallow Ego material trappings of life. This of course, is if a person does not have a personality disorder, that renders them toxic and dangerous as they will be without basic Empathy and possess no remorse, for others.

Women who have never looked their pain and their fears directly, have yet to conquer them, meaning they stay at a distance, emotionally. However, there has to be a balance between the good and bad, the light and the dark. Without fully facing the depth of tempestuous emotions that you feel toward pain and fear, you cannot possibly hope to fully envelop the deepest depths of the opposite of it. Balance in all things. The good, the love, the strength, the resiliency, all of that is at the opposite end of the pain and fear. Unless you embrace all of the bad and face it. For the greatest healing, you cannot ambition yourself to achieve the same of the good which is what makes these Dark Goddesses, and can make you, a stronger woman. As we erase all our ghosts inside, we are then blessed and granted, with the ability to guide these ghosts back to the light. You must set yourselves free in order to ascend into a new season and begin again. Persephone embodies this year after year as she ascends into a new season every spring. So must we do too.

She provides all trauma and sexual abuse survivors the Hope and Courage, to start their life fresh and anew. It is completely understandable why someone would feel that their life is destroyed and marred, and yet Persephone combined with Lilith, will help you wash those Sulphuric Blood Laden tears away and erase the emotional charge from your energy fields.

Evoking Your Inner Lioness with Sekhmet

Sekhmet is the ancient Egyptian goddess of war and destruction. Her name translates to "the powerful one". Depicted as a woman with the head of the lioness, she symbolizes destruction and rebirth. It is her husband and their son, that comprise of the triad of deities, worshiped in ancient Egypt. She is most closely connected to the Goddess of Pleasure and Luxury. The tale says that Ra, the King of the gods, was angry with humanity for their waywardness, so he ripped out his own eye and threw it at Earth. His Divine Eye transformed into Sekhmet who took on the form of a Lioness.

Whilst most people look at her as a violent Goddess, it is better known that she is a healer who would cure people for broken bones and any joint related issues. If she is not honoured properly, she can easily cause epidemics however, she would stop them as well, so long as she was given the respect that she deserved. It is through this that we learn as women to make sure that we use what inside of us to get the respect and honour that we deserve, from all of those around us, using our Dark Bold Lioness, within to show the power we have.

We too, possess the power to cause our own version of an epidemic and to stop it, them once we are honoured properly. It is Goddess Sekhmet, who is there to empower us when we are angry and to keep us from getting carried away blindly with our rage and fury. When we have old grudges from patterns that truly interfere with our ability to become successful, we have to learn to let these things go and we have to learn to work on forgiveness. The Dark Goddess teaches us that we forgive ONLY after retribution. This is not a popular afterthought in the Judeo-Christian Folklore, however it is most effective to a woman's sanity and psyche. It is through this Dark Goddess that we learn these things. She is the one there, to teach us these necessary lessons that the world wishes to keep away from us. She is the one there to teach us to let go of our anger after processing and cleansing it and forgive old wounds because joy and celebration are waiting just beyond staying stuck in negative, and low-vibratory energy fields.

Travel Your Sacred Path with Hecate

Hecate is a pre Hellenistic Goddess who carries a lit torch, to guide us through darkness and through mysterious Sacred Feminine, places. She invites us to uncover the inner magic, power, and light that we each have as women, so that we can better illuminate our path. This three headed Goddess helps each one of us to harness the lesson and awakening of the past, to understand what opportunity we have in the present, and to make the best choices for our future.

She is the queen of the darkness, a guardian of crossroads and she travels between the rounds. She protects the spells and women. Her name literally translates to "the shining one". She has long been invoked and evoked by Earth Goddesses as well as Psychic women, to show them clarity in their work and she enjoys working with Priestess energy.

She shows us that by gaining fearless dominion over everything that is dark within us, we are better illuminated by having Divine Truth. With Divine Truth we can gain access to our inner clarity, power, and wisdom. With all of this we can navigate the most treacherous of roads, and we can move forward in our lives making the best possible decisions with grace and mastery.

Consider this, every time we take action in our lives, it is because we made a decision based on information.

How many times have you looked back on a trying situation and thought to yourself "if only I had known…"?

How many times have you decided on a course of action and then in retrospect realized that if you had known everything you might have made a different choice. This is something that so many people fail to really sit with. This "I must know everything before I proceed", actually cripples people into Analysis Paralysis. People can wait for years for the "right time", but in essence, how much time do you really have?

This is very different to an inner knowing, as Hecate would say. Sometimes, we are psychically aware that a situation to manifest, is not the right time. Hence, we know that we have a Divine mission to complete, before something manifests in our life.

So much of our lives is made up of half informed decision-making. Most of the time we think we know. We think we know all the factors that are playing a role. But maybe one thing goes overlooked, maybe one thing just isn't understood. Without having all the information, we cannot possibly hope to make the best decision for our futures. If this Goddess is enveloped and what she has to teach us is truly taken to heart, this won't be an issue anymore. You need to learn to harness the lessons of your past. Just like all the other Dark Goddesses that we have come across in history, even the worst of things that happen to us comes with a lesson. We can choose to learn from everything.

Failure, for example, is not a bad thing.

So many women in particular fear failure especially in the workplace, one heavily dominated by men.

Failure simply means that you tried something. We certainly won't be perfect at everything we tried the first time. Not every decision we make is going to give us all the results that we want. There is a reason that so many people say "I made mistakes early on in my career but that I learned from them". Hecate would more than likely say that there is no such thing as Failure, simply Feedback.

You have to harness the lessons of your past. Then must examine what opportunities you have in the present but only by truly having ultimate truth can you examine the opportunities in the present in the clearest possible fashion. Taking the lessons you've learned in the past and combining them with the opportunities you are given in the present is the only way to make the best choices for your future no matter what part of your life you are trying to improve.

Destroy in Order to Create Anew with Kali

Kali's tale is that, there is no kind side to her. Her tale speaks of dancing a terrible day and bring your feet down upon the kingdoms of men. She dances on the corpse of her husband wearing a garland crafted from white skulls. She kills in fury and laps of the blood of demons. But if you want to be whole you must love her.

Kali sprang forth from the center, of a warrior goddess Durga. She sprang from the forehead in order to defeat an un-defeatable demon. She is the fiercest of goddesses, there to help us defeat the self-sabotaging patterns we create and overcome the fiercest of the unyielding demons inside. Hecate and Persephone are goddesses that we can invoke when we face dark times.

The Hindu goddess Kali is a goddess who blasts into our lives with you to prepare for or not. In fact, she will usually make her way into your life as soon as you are at the most comfortable. Once you become complacent with things as they are she will tornado into your life and flip everything upside down. It is Kali who shakes us to our core and helps us realize the frail foundation upon which we stand. This is always a very challenging lesson to learn. Just like a parent who has to teach very difficult lessons with hands-on learning, this Goddess is there to help us as we begin to mourn the ashes of all the things she destroyed, when she lends the hand lovingly, forcing us to create something new out of those actions.

There are women everywhere with self-sabotaging patterns. We are truly our own worst enemy. We judge ourselves harsher than anyone else. We criticize our mistakes, point out our flaws, and always assume that people are thinking the worst of us. Most of the time they are not. And once, we allow these self-sabotaging patterns and our inner demons to take over, it creates a vicious cycle. We stop doing things that we love, we prevent ourselves from achieving the success that we want in the workplace or at home.

We get in our own way more than anything else gets in our way. Sure, facing a dark time of tribulation can be a challenge, however we can overcome that and learn lessons from that, and then move forward. But a lower level sludge demon inside is something that continually creeps up, something that just sits there in the back of your mind, poisoning your soul and reaching your power. That is why Kali is so strong and so fierce.

She can seem like an overwhelming distraction, someone who simply comes in and destroys your world as it is. However, you have to understand, you have to take the Divine Truth that you have learned from other goddesses, so that you will appreciate that this is absolutely, necessary.

Sometimes a simple, rage-fueled **"ENOUGH"** battle cry is what it takes to halt the patterns. How many times have you been around a child or face a bad situation at work where you let things happen over and over and over, only to eventually snap and scream? This feeling of snapping is essentially what Kali rips out of us. She knows that it is deep inside of us but sometimes we have trouble accessing it. Sometimes we don't know that it is time to scream. So she steps in, and does it for us. She steps into distancing the power and the patterns of negativity after all of our patience, has gone.

Have you ever felt courage that doesn't seem like your own? We've all had our body feeling a certain way. We take an abrupt stand for ourselves and we finally quit that toxic job or separate from that unhealthy spouse, or simply free ourselves from an addiction. It is Kali who is that part of us, pushes us beyond their limits right into the darkest of years and then shows us that rather than falling we have the power to fly.

Many people are afraid of the true power of Kali. They are afraid because they know they will have to transform and change many parts of themselves, that they do not wish to look directly, at. It is only the wild woman, who has the courage to look deeply at who she is, and whom she wishes to become, that embraces Goddess Kali, in all her might.

Embracing the Dark Goddess – A Final Note

It takes great courage and tenacity to embrace the Dark Goddess Energy, when it is much easier to indulge with the sweeter, more sensual side of the Sacred Light Feminine. Yet it is during our darkest nights that we will have no greater ally than the Dark Goddess herself to bring this into the light once again. That is why we must acknowledge every aspect of the goddess in order to unleash our full Feminine Power and potential.

The Importance Difference between Feminism and Feminine Energy

It is important to address the issue of feminism versus feminine energy. We are currently surrounded by talk of third-generation feminists, young girls today in their 20s who are catching the feminist wave. I am an empowered woman however I do not support feminism. Feminism drains out of each and every one of us women our true feminine soul, our beautiful energy, and all that we can achieve in our Priestess energy. A few years ago, an article published in the New Yorker magazine where the original leaders of the feminist movement were interviewed. The comments they made were heartbreaking in a sense.

One of the issues in question talked about in this interview was in vitro fertilization. It was during a discussion about things like in vitro fertilization and couples who are having trouble conceiving that these women specifically highlighted the fact that they believed problems with conception should be treated equally between a man and woman. They believed that you shouldn't say it was one person's faults even though medically speaking there could be an issue specifically with the man or specifically with the woman. Certainly we should not blame that person as though they acted nefariously but pretending that both parties are to blame when somebody has a low sperm count or when somebody has lazy ovaries is a bit of a leap. This is what political correctness has done to today's Western Society.

These women specifically stated that science needed to develop a way for literally everything in the world to be completely equal for men and women. If a woman had to undergo in vitro fertilization to help a couple can see, the leaders of the original feminist movement believed that, men needed to be made to suffer in equal measures. Even though the issue was not with the man's body, they wanted some sort of injection to be created so that men would suffer hormonal changes or similar side effects. The entire thing fell far short of empowering women and allowing them to achieve the quality among men and instead took a very dark turn toward desiring men to suffer for no reason other than suffering.

When you really take a step back and evaluate what the original feminism idea was, you see that it tells women things like being a mother or wife or useless. It tells women that they have to get into the workplace and fight, that they have to be competitive, argumentative, and above all, masculine. I am an independent woman with my own career and a great deal of the time I work out of my home. There are things in the home that simply have to be done. Whether I live alone or with a spouse, there will be laundry to do. I have to wash clothes every day. There will be dishes to wash. I eat every day.

I happily, most days, wash dishes, sweep floors, and do laundry because it has to be done and I am home most of the day. I can simply take a five-minute break in between tasks, to transfer a load of laundry or to load some dishes. When I do this, it brings the inner peace as I work. I can focus better. Additionally, when my spouse comes home after working overtime, he has more time to spend with me because he doesn't have to do those things, which he would happily do if they needed doing. I share this because the few feminists I do know take serious issue simply at the idea of me doing dishes or laundry. Which is really unbelievable and lends a person to think that common sense has flown out of the window.

When I say that I washed two loads of laundry in one day because my spouse had training, and went to the gym and also give the yard a good clean, so there was extra laundry, they are furious. They demand, with a very odd fury, why I would do that. They want to know why I would, in their words, let the man have dominion over me or do exactly as I was told. I don't see it that way at all. These are things that simply have to be done. They are things that someone has to do one way or the other and I have no issue doing. That does not make me bold into a man. I am not taking orders. I am not expected to do these things. I simply do them because I want to.

But again, feminism has conveyed in us the idea that certain duties are considered feminine and other duties are considered masculine, and that we should hate all things considered feminine. It is this drama and confusion due to, Feminism, that makes us believe that things like washing dishes or doing laundry are viewed as the duties of a housewife, and that being a housewife is useless and lowly and therefore we should shy away from doing these activities as they are beneath us.

Those same people scoff at the notion of putting on makeup, doing their hair, or wearing something flattering to their form. In a misguided attempts to achieve equality and seek harmony between masculine and feminine poles, the same people have lost and ignored a key component to their true feminine power. The feminine energy that we have is, to some degree, tied to our sexuality which is tied inherently to looks.

I, for example, love having a strong self-worth which is supported when I choose to wear sexy lingerie under my clothes, even if no one will see it that day or when I choose to do my hair and accentuates my natural beauty with a bit of makeup. I feel better when I have sat in the sun for a few minutes soaking up vitamin D and being one with nature. None of these things am I doing for someone else.

Certainly the men in my life benefit from them because they are inherently connected to my sexuality but I do them for me, to truly achieve stronger feminine energy. This is something that all women need to appreciate.

Certainly you don't have to get all dolled up when you run to the store for a bit of milk but choosing to scowl and not do your hair or makeup and only where worn-out clothes, that don't really fit you just so that you can try and be as far from feminine as possible is not helping you but it's destroying you. It is destroying your natural self-worth as a woman.

True feminine energy is very distinct from this. Feminine energy, is all about harmony and progression with all things masculine. The female form and power is meant to be sexual, much more so than men. We are meant to have this sexual power and energy that we use complementary to our spouses, our lovers, the men in our lives. Men are not turned on by women who are dominating and masculine.

Instinctively they know something is wrong, and they are more inclined to do things like, cheat or turn to pornography as an outlet. There is a natural balance in the world's masculine and feminine energy, to be sustained. Biologically there is harmony that can be achieved between the masculine and feminine. None is better than the other.

It is feminism that is causing women to end up in miserable situations. The idea friends with benefits is really just part of masculine programming and we do it because we think we have to be strong ball busting just like men but it runs counter to our true feminine self-worth and we end up with low self-esteem, shame, stis, and more. Cultivating your true feminine energy will give you happiness, will help you to find your own strengths and to be graceful.

The female body is not the same as the male body. It's not designed to have the same level of intensity or brute force. We each have our own strengths and it is better for us to simply admit this and capitalize upon it, however to try and deny it and force ourselves to be something we aren't, isn't the business. I've been there, I've tried to convert my feminine energy into feminism years back, and what I was told I needed to be. I felt nothing but misery, bitterness, and anger. It was incredibly isolating for me. Men will avoid you like the plague, and money will certainly avoid you. Being this way doesn't get you what you truly want.

Being in touch with your feminine body, is important. A lot of women have a block in their sacral chakra, the womb area where trauma, sadness and abuse collects and send out negative signals. Addressing this darkness, this paying, and healing it will help you to overcome this struggle and to stop these negative signals from within.

You are a creator by nature. As a woman you create life. You Love in a Divine way. Women love to write, paint, dance, sing, and otherwise sculpt things out of the world that keep us one step closer to Divinity. All women struggle with their place in a masculine world sadly, and one of the best ways that you can overcome this struggle is to accept fact that your true feminine nature is the key.

Becoming more masculine will help you achieve the things you want. You may achieve them however at what cost? Accepting your feminine nature and capitalizing upon it will help you to be happy, to love, to create, and to achieve, especially money.

Feminism has told women to be equal to men but we are not meant to be equal to men. We are equal in respect to each other as energy, but women have a powerful, special, and unique energy, a feminine energy. Likewise men have their own powerful masculine energy. You don't have to fight with men to be viewed as worthy were respected. You can be a beautiful flower loving and caring with a feminine energy and it will open doors for you in all things.

Harnessing the Dark Goddess in Your Relationships

Flirting and Building Relationships: You do Not Have to be Beneath a Man

One of the biggest mistakes made by women who try to flirt with men (and start a relationship) is that they don't really take the time to first love themselves. Before you start flirting with men (whether your end goal is just that night or for the long term) you must love yourself with strong boundaries of what you will and won't tolerate. This will instill a sort of confidence that cannot possibly be faked… and men often perk up and take notice!

When you have come to this realization, you have taken the first step in becoming your best self. There is something for you to realize. You are your best self. Most women aren't good at transforming themselves into someone else. They can play the role, but it is not the true them. You aren't going to be as good as someone else as you can as be yourself. This is okay, because you have what it takes to be that magnificent woman. When you stop wasting your energy on pleasing everyone else, you are in a better position to become the best you.

You just needed to learn how to create attraction and to use the knowledge to put this confidence into your dating life.

You now have a plan of action for building the attraction. This alone is going to enhance your appeal with men. The next step is to become the best you possible and not to allow anyone to influence your self-worth.

It doesn't matter if you see the man of your dreams and he looks at you and makes rude comment. This is his perception of you and you are not responsible for how he sees you. There is no point to turning yourself into someone else for fear that you will be rejected from someone. When you realize this, you are free to express yourself, who you are, and to be a "whole" woman.

I understand that when you think "becoming whole" there is the suggestion that you are broken. **This is a false reality.** You simply must improve on certain aspects of your personality and your character which you have yet to develop and mature, because you have hidden them. The reason you've hidden them is because you have the fear of being rejected by men.

When you have hidden these traits in this situation, there are other areas of your life, as well that are equally hidden. When you are able to stop exterior things from determining how you are going to act or what part of you interacts with people, this will transform.

The best advice is to be who you are by discovering what you like, don't like, and what you will tolerate and reject. When you are who you are, you are able to accept yourself. The more you do this, the more you will become aware of yourself, and the quicker you'll master the art of being YOU. The longer that you neglect to do this, the longer that you will remain immature, timid and unrefined to those parts. When you accept all of you, you will grow and mature to become whole which is a key to capturing your self-confidence and attracting high value men.

Creating Confidence in Yourself

Before you begin flirting you must possess True Self Worth and Confidence.

DO NOT underestimate the power that being confident in yourself will have on men. It will help you to grasp flirting, instantaneously, as, you will feel confident no matter what you do, instead of shy and unsure of yourself.

Have you had the pleasure of knowing a woman that seems to have self-confidence made of steel? Think of her confidence, and ask yourself if there could be a situation where she lacked confidence. My guess is you can think of at least one.

Maybe she has all the charisma in the world in front of a crowd, but, timid in the bedroom. Or, maybe in the kitchen. Or, maybe you'd have to hang her from a cliff to find out where her lack of confidence works. HA HA ;)

There is not a single person, that doesn't have at least one area that they are completely confident in. It may be their career. Their relationship with their mother. Their hobby. Even men that can't hold a woman have one area that they have confidence in.

You may know someone that is a master in business, but a flop with the men. In business, she has all the interest of those she works with. This holds true for individuals that possess confidence in any area of their life.

Consider things in your life that you are good at. Are you good enough that you can teach them to other people? Are you able to draw another person's attention and keep them interested in with your knowledge on the subject? If so, put all doubt aside that you don't have the ability to possess magnetic confidence. The charisma is just waiting to bloom and shine.

Consider this. If you possessed the indefinite answers as to why men are attracted to women, would you have the confidence you need in your interactions with men? And, what if you understood that attraction happens and is not a choice for men. Healthy Men are attracted to High Value women, women who stand up for themselves, as Goddess Lilith did, at the dawn of time.

If you think this is an impossible concept than I'd like you to consider this: have you ever noticed all the heads of men turn as an attractive woman walks into the room? Even those with rings on their fingers or a woman sitting next to him? And, when the woman they are with, notices it, most men will respond with something like: "It's only natural."

Even the men among us that do not admit this out loud, are deeply aware that attraction is not a choice. It is physical, and at the most they can empower ourselves not to look. The fact remains, however, men are attracted to her.

Well, guess what? For women, attraction works the same way. The best part, women don't find the same things attractive as us men do. As men, what draws them, to a woman are her looks and confidence. This leaves more mature women at a disadvantage as they are older and their beauty begins to fade. This is one reason for so many women turning to cosmetic surgery.

Now, what are women mostly attracted to? Women are mostly attracted to men due to their behaviours. If you have the advantage of knowing what these behaviours are, then you will build magnetic and uncontrollable attraction with women as a man. If you were able to have the knowledge of how to tap into this would you have more confidence? Would interacting with women become that much easier?

My guess is it would be much easier. It is all a matter of knowing what works and what does not. When you have the skill and knowledge about what is effective your confidence level is that of a natural state of body and mind.

Take a deep breath and realize that you already possess all the necessary confidence, like all other women out there. Now, you need to determine what works so that you can enhance your interactions with men with confidence.

Releasing Emotional Baggage With Courage

Emotions make everyone feel vulnerable and this is why we often protect them… and rightly so. You do not want to show off your deepest emotions immediately lest someone uses them against you. Which sadly, living in a predatory world, often happens.

The other end of this is that the longer you do this—the longer you protect and hide your feminine emotions, the less in touch you may be with them. If you end up with an emotional imbalance in your life you may choose to fill it with someone else who has an abundance of emotions. This is usually how women end up dating men with emotional issues and it is never a positive situation, to be in.

You may have heard of the term "merger wish". It is a term used in psychology. What it means is that an individual attaches themselves to someone to make up for what they are missing. Some view this unhealthy attachment as love. Those that do continue to end up in codependent relationships because of this.

When you continue to attract men with emotional issues, it is likely because you haven't dealt with issues of your own. Think about it. **The common denominator in each of your relationships is you**. The sooner you are able to realize this, the more understanding you have to work on your problem.

What you must realize is that, women who refuse to tolerate dramatic men don't end up dating the man who has emotional issues. This is because they have a high value and do not allow themselves to be manipulated, under any circumstances.

When you are able to do these two things will happen:

First, men that you attract that are truly drama queens will give up and go on to a woman that they can easily control. These women are many, however, and men really don't miss out on much in terms of value.

Secondly, the men you attract, will love, honour and respect you, because you respect yourself. When you complain about a man to your friends, it makes you look dumb because after all, you have chosen to stay with him.

Men and women have a tendency to dish out the most drama that their partner will tolerate. It is just one of those quirks about humans. We seem to try to get away with the most we can.

If you happen to be a woman that isn't completely confident in yourself, men with emotional issues won't be the only thing you'll attract. You will also attract normal man who can act like drama kings (for the sake of gender argument) as well as money issues and people who take advantage of you, all the time. The men you will begin to attract, will be emotionally healthy and they will be men that treat you like you should be treated.

But the fact remains the same. In order to attract the type of person you want in your life you need to become the type of man that they are naturally attracted to. This is your only approach to attract the people you want to attract. There are not short cuts.

My guess is that this is enough to inspire you to have the courage necessary to face yourself, and that alone will empower you to become a woman of unshakable confidence.

Mastering the Fear of Rejection

Every woman fears being rejected. That is why we are too subtle with our hints and when men don't get them, we fear they rejected us and stop trying. We are afraid that if one man says no to us, it will be the ultimate failure and it will mean that no man will ever love us. But this is not true. In fact it is far from it.

What men in this situation don't realize is that when they give into the woman this is what causes the woman to reject him. She is putting him through the test to secretly determine if he is good enough and confident enough to be firm. She wants him to be confident because it makes her feel that he is strong enough to take care of her. This is a natural evolutionary process, that weeds out the emotionally weak men.

When you look at the scenario, it is an interesting one. The majority of men allow the woman to take advantage of them because they don't want to risk their relationship with her. Now, if the majority of men knew they were being tested would their fear of being rejected subside? More than likely!

What would result, would be attraction. A woman who demonstrated to the man that she has unshakable confidence and knows exactly who she is and what she deserve. His attraction would become uncontrollable. This is the main factor that women must understand when mastering the fear of rejection and getting it to work in their favor.

As a woman, you will position yourself in one of two positions. You will continue to give in with the belief that this is what your man really wants and will keep you from being rejected, or you will position yourself to stand your ground when being tested and not fold under his pressure.

The fear of rejection can work in your favor, or against you.

Now you also understand that the key to master the fear of rejection, is the same as that to build unshakable confidence: it is all about developing the ability to build attraction with a man so that you have certainty when you interact with men.

When you are in control, to be your own woman, no matter whether he likes it or not, you have reached the first principle in creating this attraction. You Like YOU!

Money and Relationships: Where they Merge

Money problems are another common issue in relationships, particularly among young couples who are just starting out in their careers. Their take-home pay might not be very high to begin with, and this problem may be made worse by poor money management skills.

The list of things that any couple might need or want to spend money on will be very long, and it can sometimes be overwhelming. It is important, however, not to deal with it, in a simplistic ad hoc basis and instead work out a proper financial plan.

The first note to make in the ledger, is, to list both of your incomes on the credit side. Then you begin the debit side. In the debit side, the first thing marked down should be ten percent of your combined incomes, which is to be set aside in a savings account for a "sunny joyous day". Remember, you're looking to attract happy days, not sad, rainy ones!

The debit side continues with all of your joint expenses which can include a home phone line or internet costs and utility costs as well as your rent or mortgage payment. Next on the list, are, any individual expenses you may have including your student loans or credit cards as well as car payments, car insurance and any other debts.

Add up both columns and deduct the debits from the credits. The difference is how much you have to spend for food and drink, gasoline and other monthly expenses.

Two simple and effective rules to keep in mind are "Don't spend money you don't have", and "Don't borrow money to back previous debts". As long as you follow these basic guidelines, you are in good shape.

Making a financial plan is a good move, even when you aren't planning on completely combining your income and expenses. At the very least, you should list all joint expenses, and also establish a budget for food and drink. This will give you an idea about how much each of you should contribute to the household fund.

You may also decide to get a joint bank account for the payment of bills and other joint expenses – if this is the case, you should set up direct deposits into the account, to ensure that your share gets paid. If you're using this or another joint account to pay for groceries and other everyday expenses, both of you should carry debit cards for the account.

It goes without saying that any optional expenses should wait until everything else mentioned above has been taken care of. If there is still some money left over at the end of the year, or at some other predetermined time, the excess funds in the joint account can be used to throw a party, place in a joint savings account (the smartest move) or buy something nice for the house.

If you failed to establish a budget plan before you began cohabitation, you may have already run up some debts that you need to handle jointly. Don't panic if this is the case – set up a plan after-the-fact and proceed as above. If the financial problems are greater than you both can cope with, consult your bank or other experts for financial advice and try to work out a feasible long-term solution.

Financial problems are a major source of stress and worry for individuals, and can put a lot of pressure on a relationship as well. Don't neglect them until it's too late.

Applying Goddess Self-Worth

People, unlike machines, don't come with user guides. Instead, we gain our early knowledge about the life's workings from our parents (and occasionally, grandparents) - people who have weathered the storms and can share the wisdom they've gained about life's various pitfalls. Parents today, though, with their attention increasingly shifting away from the household and towards more personal spheres like career and recreation, have less time to play this role for their children.

This is especially true for relationships. Today's generation, by and large, has had nobody to guide them through the many intricacies of love, lust and infatuation. As products of the sixties, a time closely associated with rebellion, self-indulgence and other excesses, their parents weren't always the best role models (to put it mildly).

The upshot of all of this is that, we now have a generation making its way through the murky realm of relationships with all the care and sophistication of an unguided missile - hurtling aimlessly towards separation, divorce and other disastrous consequences. The statistics, by now, are common knowledge: just about everybody can recall off the top of their heads that half of all marriages end in divorce, with things getting markedly worse for second and third marriages.

There is so little in the way of proper relationship guidance in this day and age that, rather than wondering why so many marriages fail, we might be better off asking why any of them succeed at all! Of course, it's not all doom and gloom – we know, after all, that love, care and passion can hold a relationship together in the face of great adversity – but even the most loving and passionate couple can only hold out so long if there are deep, persistent problems in the relationship itself.

Most couples who have been married for over two decades, will agree that maintaining their relationship is most challenging, so much so that they may have even contemplated ending their relationship at times. However, these same couples will likely also agree that there are substantial rewards in putting the effort into creating a happy and healthy relationship.

So what is the winning combination, that creates a successful relationship? Start out with commitment and dedication, plus willingness to collaborate, and even sacrifice, if necessary. Add to that the comfort of close friendship, the sweetness of passion, and the ability to focus on the light side of life and have fun. That's what it takes.

Inevitably, there will be issues in a committed relationship – some readily resolved and others that may shake it to its core. These can feel catastrophic when they occur – as if everything you were counting on has been wrenched away. This can lead to the depths of despair. Losing a committed relationship can be one of the most traumatic life events there is. What you once thought was safe and secure, can turn into a volatile mix of confusing events in which nothing seems clear or safe. You may fear that you will inadvertently do something, that will have catastrophic consequences.

You likely know what this is like if you have been in a significant relationship for some time. Even though you are one-half of a couple, you may feel all alone in your desire to stay in your relationship, particularly if your partner is no longer available to you emotionally or physically, or seems to lack a commitment to deal with the issues.

In such a situation there is both good news and bad news: it is up to you to deal with it. You may question how that can be good news. Taking responsibility for your relationship is empowering. You will discover that you are not a victim and that you have more power than you think to make a positive impact on your relationship. The important first step is to take responsibility.

Because no action exists in isolation, your every action results in a reaction. Changes you make on your own behalf will necessarily result in changes in your relationship. Therefore, the secret to a good outcome is to learn what changes you yourself can make that will spill over into your relationship.

Contrary to what we would like to think, problems in relationships always include both people....

Our first and natural inclination is to become defensive and blame our partner for the problems we are experiencing. As much as it is painful to admit, we have also had a part to play, whether or not we intended to. One person does not create problems on their own.

Let's say you are married and your husband is treating you disrespectfully. What about the bigger picture? Is this typical of how he treats others? If so, who? If it is only you who receives this treatment, that is enlightening. If that is how he consistently is in the world that is good information to know, as the odds of him treating you well are then lessened. If that is not his basic character, then in some way you are allowing him to mistreat you in that way.

This point is central to this is:

However your partner treats you, whether that is loving, kind, disrespectful, or abusive, you have taught him how to do so.

While this may seem shocking, it actually offers hope. If you take responsibility for having taught him how to treat you, you can then also take responsibility for "un-teaching" him. This may take time, but it can be done! **That does not guarantee that it will happen, as some people are not capable of sustaining a positive relationship.** In that eventuality, you are faced with the decision as to whether or not you want to continue in the relationship. I'll explore that possibility later...

Whatever the situation, hard work is involved. If you are still with me, I hope you are willing to do what it takes! The payoff of a happy relationship makes it worthwhile, right?

Although both partners are involved in relationship problems, don't take this to mean that you caused his unacceptable behavior. He must also take responsibility for his choices. If your actions to this point have not brought about the results you desire, then it is time to attempt some different strategies. Doing the same thing over and over and expecting different outcomes is crazy, so stop what you are doing and start over with some new strategies. Only then can you expect new outcomes.

Ready for exciting change and new sanity? Then let's continue....

Although this is hard to accept, the only person you can change is you!

Don't forget that.

If you have any hope that this Book will teach you how to remake your partner, or find ways to control or manipulate him, toss that false hope into the garbage. That is a dead end street.

If that doesn't work, what then?

Cultivating healthy self-worth

This main point about taking responsibility for how other people treat you does not just apply to a relationship with a lover or a spouse. Understand that no matter how people treat you, whether it is people at work, people at home, or your friends, you have to be responsible for it.

DISCLAIMER: This is not applicable when it comes to abuse. Nobody deserves abuse of any kind and certainly this entire section is only about rude or unnecessary treatment, never actual abuse.

As a woman when you have anything less than goddess level self-worth, people try to mistreat you. Nowhere is this more evident than when it comes to money and men.

When we don't opt out of situations that are negative or toxic we continue to feed it with our own life force, our own energy. Far too often people show up in our lives who think that they can just slowly erode our boundaries and that you won't do anything about it. The absolute second you feel that someone else is a negative force in your life you have to get rid of them. This could be family members who suck out all of your life force with their complaints, their selfishness, their negativity, or anything else. Misery truly loves company so individuals who have their own issues to work through might avoid working through them and instead will infiltrate your soul like a disease and make you sick. There are people who will sit and complain happily and never do anything else.

As a woman with a winning mindset, the self-confidence and self-worth of the Goddess, you no longer have to take garbage from anyone. You can distance yourself from anyone who tries to bring drama to you. You can simply ignore messages that you know will drain you.

On a personal note, I have had family members and friends involved in my life for whom I felt somewhat responsible. The nurturing side of my feminine being told me that I had to be there for them. The social requirements of supporting family at all times said that I had to help. Polite behavior stated that I was required to respond to each message and pick up the phone for every phone call. Unfortunately, these were people who had very serious demons, would never face the depths of their fears or their issues, never tried to better themselves or fix themselves. They were perfectly content making simple mistakes like complaining about people to third parties like myself rather than complaining to the person with whom they had an issue. Such simple things were draining the life force that I had.

I had an emotional bank and these people made far too many withdrawals and never enough deposits. It dawned on me once that these same people would simply call me and spend 30 minutes straight complaining about what eventually seems like the exact same issues in their lives. Not once during that phone call that they asked me about how I was. Some went even further and would complain that they miss me and I have never come to visit and yet they would never visit me and when I offered they would complain that they were too busy and I should be the one to go out of my way. Finally, there were those "friends" who once a year or so when send a message to see how I was but were really trying to maintain a healthy relationship with me. I was willing to accept the correct use of excuses, I was willing to let people overstep my personal boundaries all because I truly thought that I was a bad person and especially a bad woman, if I wasn't there for them when I had no excuse not to be. My own health and well-being and self-worth didn't seem a legitimate excuse. Something I had to learn somewhat later in life was to apply the same concepts that are taught on an airplane to my life:

You have to put the mask over yourself before you assist anyone around you.

You cannot be of any use to anyone if you do not secure yourself first. If you let people use you, if you let people bring their garbage or drama to your door and you don't distance yourself, they will continue to do it. You are responsible for yourself. You are responsible for your own emotional health. There are people who will happily drain you emotionally until there is nothing left if you don't put an end to it.

You need to understand your true goddess level self-worth so that you can stop accepting these crappy excuses, stop letting people step over you, and stop keeping people in your life who don't give you any good reason to do so. You need to learn to listen to the Goddess inside of you, the one who is trying to give you foresight and intuition, the one who is trying so desperately to help you ask the question, **"What does this person really want from me?"**

You do not owe anything to anyone. Everybody wants something and if the interactions you are having with people are not healthy, stop them. Whether this is a relationship, friends, family, colleague, or anyone else, you are the one who teaches people how to treat you. You teach people what things you will tolerate and what things you won't. You teach people what stupid behaviour you accept and what things you refuse to let into your life. You on your own are capable of creating a worthy, beautiful, and stable version of yourself so long as you do not let past experiences prevent you from shining. Let people around you know what you are comfortable with, let them know that they cannot overstep those boundaries. You cannot command a life full of happiness both financially and sexually if you are afraid to express your true opinions.

I eventually learned how to achieve Goddess level self-worth. I put my foot down and alleviated that social context of guilt that had kept me involved in such toxic situations for so long. I had one family member in particular who would call and complain without any introduction. And once they were done complaining they would ask how I was but not before legitimately telling me, "I'm going to mute the phone because I'm blow drying my hair but you can keep talking". Instinctively this upset me. I justified the behavior for so long because I figured that they probably just needed someone who assists them, and helps them for the time. This was a long time ago, and nowadays I would never entertain someone that just wished to drain me.

It didn't take long to for me to realize that I was going out of my way to justify crappy behavior from someone else, someone who should theoretically love me as much as I love them. But I had taught them this behavior by not stopping it when it first started. Better late than never is absolutely true.

They didn't quite get it. They said things like, "Don't worry. I am still listening" or "no, it's fine". It only took two or three times hanging out before that family member started to say, "You can call me back if you want because I have to blow-dry my hair". It was a much longer road to repair the treatment I had allowed to grow that it would've been if I can simply stop that treatment early on.

It took months of my personal suffering and life force being sucked out of me before I put my foot down and said that I no longer cared about being viewed as selfish or having any of those negative stereotypes associated with me simply because I was a woman who decided to care for myself and know my self-worth. A man who put his foot down as a strong man and people respected him for that but when I put my foot down I got a slew of insults.

But having true goddess self-worth means you don't care about those things because you know what is really important. You know that you deserve healthy relationships of all kinds.

Applying Lessons from the Dark Goddess in Your Career and with Your Money

We Don't Need to Act like Men to Be Successful

Women are notorious for not making the same big money than men do. Even if you do manage to make good money in the corporate world you are considered a "bitch". This is a terrible message. Men who are strong, independent, and demand respect our people to be feared, people that we set up as role models. Women who do the exact same thing are called terrible names. A man who gets upset over something being mishandled is a good leader, a good employee but a woman who gets upset is considered too emotional and no doubt every man in the workplace thinks a joke relating to hormones. This environment is toxic for feminine energy. Traditional corporations thrive on the masculine energy of competing, dominating, and belittling or humiliating those around you so you can win. Some might argue that women are too weak or pathetic to handle such a bullying culture.

The message here is one that women have to start acting like men, taking on those same characteristics in order to make money. This conveys the idea that women have to be rude or disrespectful to other women in order to get ahead. But screw that. The real feminine power doesn't come from belittling other women were competing against them. There is enough room for success for all women. The real feminism, the true ideas of being a successful female embodying both light and dark, suggests that we have to help one another. We can all succeed.

Women everywhere can make the same big money, can get the same positions, and can start the same companies without having to step on the faces of other women to do so. We have the power to change the corporate world. We have the power to make the same money. We can keep our dignity and handle the same money that men receive without becoming a fully. The greatest embodiments of the dark Goddess throughout different cultures have shown us that women have such great potential without having to step on other women. Women achieve great things by not succumbing to a male-dominated world and simply helping other women.

There are things that hold women back though. Most of the time we don't make the big money that men make, because money is masculine. We struggle with the masculine energy involved with money. We don't feel safe generating such large amounts of income either. Society encourages us to remain small, after all if we become successful and somehow we are responsible for belittling or emasculating men all around us. Don't fall for this lie. **Have the self-esteem necessary to become the greatest woman you can possibly be**. Let the Dark Goddess speak and act through you, using you as a pillar for success.

Study Finance from a Feminine Point of View

Women also fail to take the time to study finances in a feminine form. Women replicate what other women do by fighting for money in a masculine way. You can attract money in some of the same ways that men do while still making that attraction feminine, in its nature. Do not be afraid of true money. Money won't change you as long as you stay true to who you are.

It is the softer part of our feminine nature that causes us to give things away a lots and to do things as favours. We might do the exact same thing that a man does for a friend or a colleague and when offered recompense we turn it down out of politeness or meekness. A man would accept without question. And this man would be respected for doing that. We, on the other hand, are expected to turn it down. When it comes time to making a living at what you love to do you might have hesitated, frozen, been afraid to ask for what you know you deserve.

A lot of women don't bring up the subject of what they charge even though deep inside they have an expectation of what they expect to be given in return for their services. And yet if you do this, you won't get what you want because you don't ask for it at the beginning. **The root cause of this is low self-esteem.** Most women simply hate parts of themselves and this is an inner demon, that makes it nearly impossible to generate money the way that a man would. Nothing determines your work for you. You have to determine it. You have to be honest with yourself and accept only what you know you are worth.

Building your financial self-worth comes from truly basing your lower level demons, letting the dark Goddess give you the power to overcome that self-doubt and to truly assess what it is you are worth and no turning back down when it does not meet your expectations, is not a bad thing. When men sit around and turn down job after job because it simply doesn't pay them what they know they are worth, they are considered strong. **You are no less of Strength.** Do not let men bring you down by offering a lower amount than you know you are worth. Don't accept it. Be strong and firm in your convictions. Once you have assessed what you are worth, make sure everyone knows it and make sure that you get it. When you do this, it will surprise you how often people are perfectly happy to meet your demand.

Changing the Wage Gap

On average, it takes women 10 years more to earn a man's pay. The typical 20-year-old female who starts a full-time position today will make roughly $418,800 less than her average male counterpart at the end of a 40 year career. In order to make up this difference and close that wage gap, women have to work 10 years longer than men. That's not even the worst of it. The pay gap for women compared to women who are black, Latino, Asian, or any other women of colour, is even worse when stood alongside their white counterparts. No matter how you slice it women are still coming up short. Women are paid less than men, a single woman with kids paid less than the male counterpart. Women between the age of 45 and 64 are paid $.72 for every dollar that men make. Even young women are being paid $.91 on the dollar compared to men.

Today women are simply paid less the same amount of work. This is a serious problem when you consider fields like Doctors or computer programmers. Even in low-wage occupations like, fast food or childcare women still make less than their men. Study after study shows that, conscious and unconscious stereotypes are what keep women earning less. If a hiring manager looks at two identical resumes, one with the name Jennifer and one with the name John, they will offer the male applicant a salary roughly $4000 more than they would offer the female applicant and they think that the male applicant is more competent. There was literally no reason for this other than one was a male and one was a female.

But not all of the onus is placed on hiring managers for social stereotypes. One of the key reasons that women make less than men is simply because they don't negotiate the same way. Even if that same John and Jennifer were to be offered separate salaries with a $4000 difference, Jennifer could easily negotiate for higher pay. Of course not knowing what the offer was for John makes it a bit difficult to realize that you're being shafted, but knowing your work and how to go she the same way and to, by capitalizing upon the powers of the Dark Goddess, you can refine your skills.

Let's look at a business negotiation example so that you can get a better insight into exactly how the spirit of goddesses like Lilith can be channeled into better negotiations for you. Understand that these are all true examples of real women just like you who can utilize the power of the dark goddesses to help them achieve goals in business.

The example is this: a founder for a big grocery store chain had a hard time getting a loan for business when she wanted to open the first three stores. Banking is an industry dominated by males. It is an industry where the idea of masculine power and money are reinforced regularly. A female founder finds her requests for a loan, only triggered these masculine stereotypes. It was only through her fourth round of negotiations that the ambiguity had been reduced on both sides of the negotiating table. The entrepreneur better understood how this process works, the bank was impressed by her track record. She was able to bargain in different contexts because she had developed negotiation skills that accommodated different bargaining styles and different cognitive biases that might be present at the negotiation table.

Another example: during a negotiation situation, gender triggers you a superior performance by female negotiators. A leader within the advertising industry actually spoke about her early days working in her firm. When she started out her male colleagues would ask her to take part in their pitches. She would give them ideas and they would present them. Once the idea was selected they actually credited her with their success.

There are a lot of factors that affect your negotiation success. No matter how talented you might be, no matter how many women enter into historically male industries, equalizing opportunities doesn't just fall on one person's shoulders. You cannot simply wait around for a male-dominated industry to start respecting you as a woman. Goddess Lilith did not wait around for Adam to respect her as an equal. She simply refused to be dominated, and left. Through this refusal, she gained a great deal of her power. As a woman in business you need to understand not only how to demand your work but how to negotiate in all situations for better respect, for better pay, for better benefits, for better or whatever it is. Men will typically revisit, the pay and the position they have after, great success in a company. They are encouraged to do this.

For example, a man who started off as an intern was promoted to assistant during which time, he spent a great deal of his efforts reading over scripts in Hollywood and finding those which will work while for his bosses to read. Eventually his bosses had a great track record of selecting the scripts he sent their way and converting them into movies. Looking over how much money they had made based on the script he had spent, he approached his bosses one day and asked for meeting. During that meeting he asked that they give him a higher salary within reason and a new job title. His position and responsibilities changed very little but he went from being a regular assistant to an executive assistant and eventually to an executive producer. Each of these changes to his position title warranted more respect in the outside world and more income within the company. **This man is no different from you or myself.** Any woman can do just that. But sometimes we get in our own way. Sometimes we let things like self-doubt or demons interfere with our ability to succeed. That is why channeling Goddess Empowerment, can help you to achieve all things.

The Dark Goddess is there for you, ready and waiting to help you become the woman that you are meant to be. The Dark Goddess awaits you to receive her and begin to channel all the strength, power, fear, and darkness that she has to offer, recognizing that these traits while dark, are not bad. These traits counterbalance the softness and the sensuality that comes with the good. These traits are what give you the power to negotiate the same way that the women in these examples negotiated.

That first example where the female store owner had to wait until her third store to really get a handle on things is a perfect example of how the dark Goddess teaches us to learn from our mistakes, to take lessons from the past. We use those lessons and combine them with the opportunities we have in the present just like she did on her fourth store.

The Dark Feminine

What is the dark feminine? We talked so much about the dark Goddess and channeling the power of the dark Goddess.

The dark feminine is a lustful, passionate, seductive, strong, courageous, angry woman comfortable with the true nature of turning an average person into a goddess.

Today we live in a society where we tell children from a very young age that they can be anything they want yet, many of the words used to describe the dark feminine are things we are told to avoid, things we are told not to be. Many religions tell us that women who are shameful or unclean have to be hidden because they are nothing but bad people who evoke lust. Well sure, when you put it like that it sounds terrible. And that is exactly why the end up with people were sexually repressed.

You want sex. That is perfectly natural. However, as a woman you are told that you were dirty, nasty, that something is wrong with you if you desire sex.

Those people were told to apologize for their sexual desire are the ones who turned into sexual deviants. The dark Goddess Lilith does not want us to be sexual deviants. The dark Goddess once limited to the wild, women cannot be tamed and therefore cannot be shamed, women who know that there's nothing wrong with them for wanting and using their sexual nature.

In order to become connected to the dark feminine, you have to look at the parts of yourself that you were told your entire life to repress, in order to better fit into society. You have to remember the wilderness inside of you. You should never dim your light to please others. You should never dim yourself to make other people feel better.

As a dark feminine woman never hesitate to use whatever means you have to deliver justice to yourself and to those who you love.

There is a very important elements that the dark Goddess wants conveyed: so many women today find themselves financially beholden to men. This could stem from simply never being told that they could make money for themselves, from growing up in a society where they are supposed to be inferior, or anything else. When we face challenging financial circumstances and they have nowhere else to run, we will endure more of abuse. There is a reason so much of what is talked about focuses on money. Money is the key to safety and independence in this world.

We live in a world where women are suffering and there's nothing they can do about it because they are financially unable. That is why you need to work on your wealth so that you can be safe and independent. Shy away from being a timid or quiet woman. Behave like the Goddess you are and achieve great things.

Liberating Your Dark Feminine

If you want to attract money like a magnet, to enjoy success in your finances in the workplace, liberate your dark feminine. How do you do this? Focus on your sacred *yoni*, your sacred vagina.

Don't freak out.

You might be a bit confused as to what a vagina has to do with money. Well, it actually has what to do with money and not in the sense of prostitution. As a woman you get a lot of mixed messages about money. But you also mixed messages about your sexuality and they actually are parallel messages.

We are told by society not to want sex. We are told that we should show our pleasure and we shouldn't have too many orgasms. We should embrace our sexuality. Likewise, we are told that we shouldn't want money too much. We shouldn't show how much we love money.

Well it is time to give these notions a middle finger.

In fact, it is time to change the way you carry your thoughts about money and orgasms. Think of them as the same.

The faster and easier you climax, the more money you can bring into your home. When you orgasm your mind reaches an altered state, a sort of trance and you get affirmations that manifest exactly what you want in that moment. Women always struggle with being a radiant, passionate, and lustful woman. When you liberate your dark feminine you get to love your seductive side and your femininity. You get to own your feminine energy and enjoy the flow it has. You will notice that once you do this, once you are no longer afraid to show people that you are sexual, you are tackling the inner demons of self-hate and repression that society plants inside of you. You are allowing the dark Goddess to help you overcome the struggles and to liberate who you are meant to be.

Your feminine vessel should be open, receiving, impregnated. You need to receive money. Money is masculine and money wants to provide for you. With more balance in your sexual energy you will find it easier to receive money. Money and sex stem from the same chakra, the same route. So when you balance money and sex you can get your creative juices flowing, pun intended.

We have talked before about the second chakra and the fact that it is blocked for many women. When you balance your energy between money and sex and let them work in tandem you find a better balance in the rest of your life and you will be able to identify the issues you are having with your second chakra and fix them. Once you learn how to use your money energy you get to experience a brand-new level of Goddess power.

To do this focus on the Dark Feminine Goddesses that we've talked about, learn from those women who are comfortable with the darkest depth of their sex, their obsession, their lust, and their power. Do not fear the dark feminine goddesses. The light feminine is important but it is not everything. The light feminine is certainly important to you are as a woman, but without the dark feminine to balance all things, you will never reach your full potential.

Dark Feminine Energy, Sexuality, and Money: How it Ties Together

Empowered Goddess energy, in connection with your dark feminine energy, means you need to deeply address healthy money flow, great sex, and overall empowerment. So many of these facets are connected and yet we tried to separate them. We try to sift the sexuality and sensuality out of everyday life when realistically it should be present and you should be comfortable with it. Many women don't voice what they believe because they view this as a masculine characteristic when in reality it is far from it. Feminine Goddess Empowerment is a deep, dark and seductive energy that runs within each one of us. You need to be comfortable with the sexual element of anything and encourage or empower yourself to find that within. This is an honour. Many women fail to realize that in order to be in flow with your money, to reach that level of career and financial success, you need to be comfortable with that dark and seductive energy have. This is what makes you whole. You cannot possibly achieve the greatest successes in life if you're only half of your potential.

Your entire potential embodies the dark and the light.

You need to find the courage to stand up for who you are, what you are, and all aspects of that. You don't need to copy the style of someone else, you need to create your own.

You might wonder why so much of sexuality and money is linked in this book but the reason for that is that women who are exceptionally comfortable with their sexuality wield a great deal of financial power. Money and sex originate from the same place and we try to suppress the sexuality in us that actually empowers us.

The more creative energy you put into yourself, the more you will start to turn yourself on. This might sound silly at first, however, if you really pay attention and you focus on your body you will notice that your libido gets higher as you start to embrace your feminine energy. The more that you focus on yourself, finding yourself, creating, and being all that you can be, the more feminine energy will have. This energy is mysterious, cool, and invigorating. You will truly fall in love with yourself in a way that you previously didn't think possible. More importantly, men will start to work for your attention.

Men are meant to work for our attention. We should not work for theirs. When women try to behave in a masculine way, something we talked about with the confusion among feminism, you end up doing what a man is supposed to do. Men are supposed to chase up. The same lessons can be applied to money. We do very odd things to attract money when we start to take on masculine traits because we simply forget the power of our feminine sexuality and the ties it has to money.

The biggest mistake we make is to start selling off our self-worth.

Your self-worth stems from you. This is a non-negotiable item. Either people treat you with respect or they don't.

With that said, as you start to cultivate more of your feminine power think about what you do before you react and have the courage to take a moment alone with your emotions. This will make you more attractive to money because you will truly find yourself in a position where you don't desperately need money all the time. It can be incredibly challenging to break out of this limiting mindset but once you do you won't feel so lost and empty on the inside as you won't be succumbing to that masculine mad dash for money. Instead you will open yourself up to receive it.

Never sell off your self-worth out of desperation, for money.

Conclusion

Now you have the tools to start embracing your Dark Feminine, discovering your feminine energy and applying it to your life. There's so much to learn from each of these goddesses, so many opportunities to channel what they have and use that energy and knowledge to prepare for the future. Study always, seek regular improvements and never compromise your self-worth. Use the dark feminine to enhance your sexuality, return to the wild, never be ashamed of who you are. Open yourself up as the vessel you are and wait to be filled with knowledge, power, and money. Keep yourself and those you love safe and independent by becoming a strong-willed, dark Goddess yourself.

Made in the USA
Middletown, DE
13 June 2019